WILD ABOUT ANIMALS

RED PANDAS

By Martha London

Kaleidoscope
Minneapolis, MN

BIGFOOT BOOKS

The Quest for Discovery Never Ends

This edition first published in 2020 by Kaleidoscope Publishing, Inc.

No part of this publication may be reproduced in whole or in part without written permission of the publisher.

For information regarding permission, write to Kaleidoscope Publishing, Inc.
6012 Blue Circle Drive
Minnetonka, MN 55343

Library of Congress Control Number
2019938855

ISBN
978-1-64519-009-7 (library bound)
978-1-64494-251-2 (paperback)
978-1-64519-109-4 (ebook)

Printed in the United States of America.

FIND ME IF YOU CAN!

Bigfoot lurks within one of the images in this book. It's up to you to find him!

TABLE OF
CONTENTS

CHAPTER 1

Picky Eaters

The moon shines down over the forest. Stars speckle the sky. The red panda is ready for a snack. He was curled up on a tree branch. But he needs to get down to get some food.

The red panda is a picky eater. He eats bamboo. But he doesn't like the woody stuff. The red panda prefers the bamboo leaves. He will also eat the shoots if they are tender.

FUN FACT

Red pandas make a twittering sound to each other when they want to mate.

Red pandas spend most of
their time in the trees.

Red pandas use their claws to climb trees.

The red panda starts the climb down from his fir tree. He climbs down headfirst. The red panda uses his sharp claws. His claws dig into the tree bark. He jumps onto a lower branch. Red pandas have excellent balance.

His fluffy ringed tail waves behind him. The red panda makes his way to the forest floor in the dark.

He pads across the soft ground on his big paws. Leaves and pine needles litter the forest floor. The red panda moves quietly.

PARTS OF A
RED PANDA

red fur for
camouflage

tail for balance
and warmth

sensitive ears

bowed legs for walking
on branches

claws for climbing

Red pandas eat 2 to 4 pounds (1 to 2 kg) of bamboo a day. That's 20 to 30 percent of their body weight!

A bamboo **grove** is in front of the red panda. He sits near a few young plants. The red panda has an extra-long wristbone. It acts like a thumb. He uses it to grab the bamboo shoots. The red panda pulls the leaves off first. Leaves have the most **nutrients** for the red panda. Then he moves on to the narrow shoots.

After his meal, the red panda climbs back up a tree. His claws hook into the bark. He scales up the side and onto a branch. The red panda can use the branches like a ladder. He likes to be high up.

CHAPTER 2

Blending In

Snow covers the pine trees in the forest. Up in the branches, something moves. It's hard to see. The red panda has excellent **camouflage**. Her fur is the same red-brown color as the tree bark. This keeps her safe from **predators**. Predators cannot see her from the ground. Even the white part of her face blends in. Her white spots look like snow.

Red pandas' thick fur protects them from the cold.

Red pandas blend into trees.

ARE RED PANDAS RELATED TO GIANT PANDAS?

Red pandas aren't related to giant pandas. Scientists have had a hard time classifying red pandas. Red pandas have features in common with many different animals. In the past, scientists have grouped red pandas with giant pandas and raccoons. Now they are in their own family.

Red pandas are used to the cold. They live in mountain ranges in southern China. High in the mountains, snow is common. But this red panda likes the cold. She has thick fur to keep her warm.

She curls up in the tree. Her long tail wraps around her. It is like a blanket. She buries her nose under her tail. The red panda is cozy. She's going to take a long nap.

FUN FACT
The red panda is also called the cat-bear, firefox, and Himalayan raccoon.

A red panda's tail can be like a blanket.

Red pandas don't **hibernate**. But their bodies do slow down. The red panda doesn't need to eat as much in the cold weather. She saves up her energy. The red panda gets up and moves around a little bit. But she explores much less than in warm weather. There is also less of her favorite food. Bamboo leaves are hard to find in the winter. She can eat the stalks. But they are not as tasty. And they have fewer nutrients than the leaves.

Red pandas stay active during the winter.

HOW BIG ARE
RED PANDAS?

Red pandas can grow up to 3.8 FEET (1.2 M) long!

6 feet (1.8 m)

3.8 feet (1.2 m)

15

CHAPTER 3

Red pandas listen for danger in the trees.

At Home in the Trees

A loud sound startles the red panda. He scurries up the tree. His claws dig into the bark. He is a fast climber. The red panda feels safest in trees. He does not have a lot of defenses. His claws are sharp. But he is not a fighter. The best thing for him to do is avoid danger.

The best place to avoid danger is in the tall tree branches. He spends most of his days in the treetops. The red panda was born in the trees. He was born to be a climber. His front legs are **bowed**. This allows his big paws to grip the tree branches more easily.

The branch the red panda is on right now is wobbly. It sways as he looks at the distance to the next branch. His tail balances him. He can leap more than 5 feet (1.5 m). When he lands on the branch, it bounces. Again, his tail steadies him. The pine needles rustle. He walks along the narrow branch. When he reaches the trunk, he climbs to a higher limb.

FUN FACT
A red panda's diet is 95 percent bamboo.

Red pandas have bowed legs to help them stay on branches.

Safely out of harm's way, he perches in the tree. His ears perk up. He hears some more rustling. But it is just a bird. Red pandas like to be alone. This red panda doesn't spend a lot of time with other red pandas. He mates with a female once a year. Then he leaves. The female red panda raises the cubs by herself.

Right now, it's the middle of summer. Mating season won't come until early winter. The morning's excitement wore the red panda out. He lies down on his tree branch. His legs hang down over the sides. The red panda closes his eyes. It's time for a nap.

Trees make the perfect bed for red pandas.

CHAPTER 4

People destroy red panda habitats.
But other people help them.

Status: Endangered

Farms spread out across the landscape. Chainsaws grind and whine in the early hours of the morning. Trees crash to the ground. **Deforestation** means the red panda's **habitat** gets a little smaller. He lives in a unique habitat. The red panda needs forests and lots of bamboo. If the forests are destroyed, he does not have anywhere to go. Red pandas are **endangered.** The red panda goes farther into the forest. He doesn't like the sound of the chainsaws.

Lately, the red panda has noticed more people in his forest. But they don't carry loud chainsaws. They are quiet. Sometimes they point at him. He watches them. If they move too fast, he scurries to another tree. But mostly they stick to themselves. Sometimes they plant bamboo. The red panda really likes that. Bamboo grows quickly. That means more food for him.

FUN FACT
Red pandas can live up to fifteen years in the wild.

Where Do Red Pandas Live?

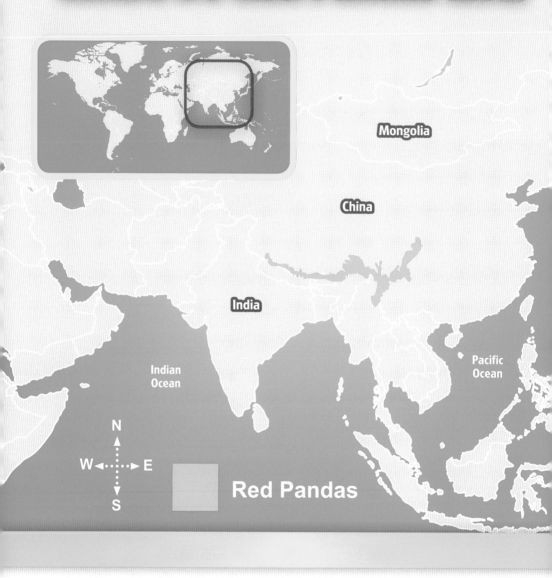

Mongolia

China

India

Indian Ocean

Pacific Ocean

N
W ◄····►E
S

Red Pandas

Some red pandas live in zoos. Red pandas are protected, but **poaching** is still a problem. Zoos keep a population of red pandas safe. They can be reintroduced into the wild. Many zoos have captive breeding programs.

The red panda gives birth in the early spring. Her enclosure is indoors. She stays away from guests when she raises her cubs. The red panda makes a nest. She finds a hole in a tree in her indoor enclosure. She gathers moss. The moss makes a soft place for her cubs.

Red pandas are shy.

The red panda has two cubs. She is used to being handled. People come into her enclosure. They wear gloves. The gloves smell bad. The people pick up her cubs and look at them. But as long as the cubs are healthy, the people put them back in the nest. The mother gives her cubs a bath. She needs to wash the smell from the gloves off.

Red pandas are endangered. But many people try to help them. Some take care of the forests where they live. Some protect them in zoos. They want to make sure red pandas will be around for years to come.

FUN FACT
Red pandas only weigh up to 20 pounds (9 kg)!

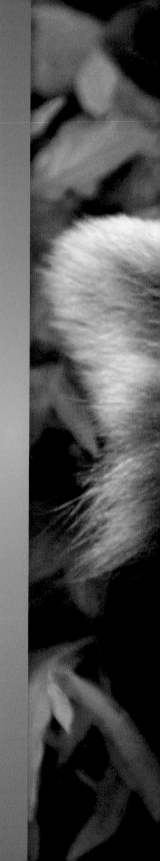

Zoos help the public learn about red pandas.

BEYOND
THE BOOK

After reading the book, it's time to think about what you learned.
Try the following exercises to jumpstart your ideas.

THINK

DIFFERENT SOURCES. Think about what types of sources you could find on red pandas. What could you find in an encyclopedia? What could you learn at a zoo? How could each of the sources be useful in its own way?

CREATE

SHARPEN YOUR RESEARCH SKILLS. Red pandas are threatened by poachers. Other animals are also harmed by poaching. Where could you go in the library to find more information about poaching? Who could you talk to who might know more? Create a research plan. Write a paragraph about your next steps.

SHARE

SUM IT UP. Write one paragraph summarizing the important points from this book. Make sure it's in your own words. Don't just copy what is in the text. Share the paragraph with a classmate. Does your classmate have any comments about the summary? Do they have additional questions about red pandas?

GROW

REAL-LIFE RESEARCH. What places could you visit to learn more about red pandas? What other things could you learn while you were there?

RESEARCH NINJA

Visit *www.ninjaresearcher.com/0097* to learn how to take your research skills and book report writing to the next level!

RESEARCH

DIGITAL LITERACY TOOLS

SEARCH LIKE A PRO
Learn about how to use search engines to find useful websites.

FACT OR FAKE?
Discover how you can tell a trusted website from an untrustworthy resource.

TEXT DETECTIVE
Explore how to zero in on the information you need most.

SHOW YOUR WORK
Research responsibly—learn how to cite sources.

WRITE

GET TO THE POINT
Learn how to express your main ideas.

PLAN OF ATTACK
Learn prewriting exercises and create an outline.

DOWNLOADABLE REPORT FORMS

Further Resources

BOOKS

Franchino, Vicky. *Animal Camouflage*. Scholastic, 2016.

Gish, Melissa. *Red Pandas*. Creative Education, 2018.

Gregory, Josh. *Red Pandas*. Scholastic, 2016.

WEBSITES

FACTSURFER

Factsurfer.com gives you a safe, fun way to find more information.

1. Go to www.factsurfer.com.

2. Enter "Red Pandas" into the search box and click 🔍.

3. Select your book cover to see a list of related websites.

Glossary

bowed: When something is bowed, it is curved. Red pandas have bowed legs that allow them to balance in trees.

camouflage: Camouflage allows an animal to blend into its surroundings. Red pandas have red fur that acts as camouflage.

classifying: Classifying is the process scientists use to group animals together. Scientists had a hard time classifying red pandas.

deforestation: Deforestation is the removal of trees that destroys animal habitats. Deforestation destroys red panda habitats.

endangered: A species is endangered when its population in the wild is very low. Red pandas are endangered because of deforestation.

grove: A grove is a group of trees growing together. A bamboo grove is a perfect place for a red panda to find a meal.

habitat: A habitat is a place where animals live. A red panda's habitat has lots of bamboo to eat.

hibernate: To hibernate means to go into a long sleep to save energy. Red pandas do not hibernate in the winter.

nutrients: Food has nutrients that give animals energy. Bamboo leaves have the most nutrients for the red panda.

poaching: Poaching is illegal hunting of protected animals. Poaching hurts red panda populations.

predators: Predators are animals that hunt and eat other animals. Red pandas stay in the trees to hide from predators.

Index

ABOUT THE AUTHOR

Martha London lives in Saint Paul, Minnesota. She writes children's books full time. When she isn't writing, you can find her hiking in the woods.